# Dark and Theatrical
## A Poetic Odyssey

## Gabriel Mero

Pages Promotions, LLC
Birmingham, Michigan
**www PagesPromotions com**
Info@PagesPromotions com
(2021) Gabriel Mero

Print ISBN: 978-1628282436
E-Book ISBN: 978-1628282443
LOCCN: 2021909353

## *DEDICATION*

For the guy who broke my heart...

...and the one who
put it back together

# Table of Contents

Gabriel Mero

Gabriel Mero

----

# *PART ONE: DARK*

----

# *Lachrymosa*

---

If I died tomorrow, would anyone notice?
If I finally gave up the will to live
Or decided to end it, would it matter?
Would you regret the invisible scars
You heartily carved into my tender flesh?
Would you acknowledge the pain
You so carelessly inflicted?
I truly believe that some of you care
No one cares enough
Not 'til it's too late

---

Gabriel Mero

# *Hiding*

There are so many things that I hide behind a smile
Cleverly disguise with a well-timed joke
From the outside, I'm sure my life seems charmed
Like I enjoy a privileged existence – free of worry
Some would say that I lack responsibility
And just overdramatize to garner sympathy
I'm grateful for the people who have seen the truth
And have stuck by me, trying their best to offer support
To take on the impossible task of building me up
I know it's not easy to love someone like me
How exhausting it is to constantly have to reassure me
I'm hyper-aware of the burden I place on others
The guilt weighs so heavily on me at all times
I wish I could be low maintenance
That caring for me wasn't such a tribulation
I overcompensate by being extremely loyal
And ridiculously generous,  but it's not enough
Eventually, everyone gets tired of it and leaves
I should be used to it by now,
This is how it's always been
But each abandonment smarts worse than the last
I've gotten good at hiding the pain

# Fractured Heart

I am the guy you hook up with, not fall for
The guy you string along
Because your options are scarce
I am the guy you decide would be better as a friend
than a lover
The guy you use to see that your needs are met
Why am I trapped in this eternal cycle of
Disappointment and devastation?
Why am I never good enough to make it official?
Why am I your emotional punching bag,
Your therapist and savior?
I used to believe that if I kept trying, someone good
would come along
Not to rescue me from any pit of despair, but to make
Me forget the pain ever existed
With each new heartbreak, I lose more of myself,
Give less of myself
Is there even anything left here? Anything worth loving?
I try so hard to get it right, but in the end,
It's never enough  I am never enough
How long can a fractured heart keep beating
Until it just gives up?

Gabriel Mero

# Razor's Edge Ballet

I dance around this razor's edge as skillfully as a trained
Ballet dancer
The sharpness scares me, but I manage it avoid it
Completely
If I keep up this façade of confidence, keep my
Attention fixed on the task
I can keep this charade forever—at least that's what
I tell myself
This constant flurry of activity leaves me exhausted
To the bone
And yet, when the opportunity arises, sleep stubbornly
Will not come
There really is no rest for the wicked
I know it's only a matter of time until my concentration
Slips, 'til I take a wrong step
And teeter over the edge into the coldness,  entirely
Devoid of color, of meaning
When that time comes, will I readily accept my fate
Or will I plummet to my death wishing I had been
Stronger?

Gabriel Mero

# *Going Under*

The water laps at my face, threatening to stifle my
Breath
It's icy cold, like a million pin pricks all over my body
I want to breathe, want to survive
But the weight is pulling me down
The more I fight to free myself
The more I feel myself falling
If only someone cared enough
To try to save me
But this is my isolation
I'm going under

# The Warrior

The darkness hovers at the edges of my periphery
Always there, always waiting to descend
It's got me locked in a macabre game of
Hide and seek
Stalking me like a hunter does its prey
Occasionally I allow myself to ponder
What it would feel like to acquiesce
To surrender totally and let it wash over me
I've fought so hard for too long to keep
This beast at bay, to stave off the inevitable
It's exhausting, this incessant battle
A little peace would be nice, refreshing
Contrary to belief, there is a grace in defeat, an honor
The offer is tempting, I can't deny that
But I was not conditioned to succumb
I will wage this war until my dying breath
I will not let the darkness reign supreme
Not while I possess even an ounce of strength
My body may be weak and feeble
But my soul is that of a warrior

# *Disappear*

There is a thought that often slips into my mind, dark,
Theatrical, and unbidden
If I were to disappear, would anybody really notice?
Would they even care?
It seems that the people with which I surround myself
Care for me only when I serve a purpose
Too many hungry hands outstretched, desperate to
Take anything and everything they can

My once sturdy foundation is cracked; it has
Weathered too many storms, suffered a lack of
Maintenance for far too long
One day it will collapse, and I can't help but wonder
Who will care?
Who will be there to sift through the rubble
And help build me back up?
Is my only reason for existing to be helpful to others?
Am I forever doomed to give, but to never receive
Anything in kind?
What would happen if I stopped?
Would there be anything exceptional about me then?
Would I have anyone to care even in the slightest?
Would I be cast aside like a childhood toy
Long outgrown?

These thoughts reverberate in my head, eternally, often
Blocking out other thoughts
What is wrong with me that no one can care about me

For me, not for what I can do for them?
They say it's better to give than to receive, and I agree
Whole-heartedly
But how long can I give without getting something
Back?
How much of me can I give until there is simply nothing
Left?
In the end, will I be the one to deal the devastating
Blow, or will it be someone else?
If my walls were thicker, would I be better suited to
Weather the storm?
I can hide these inner demons with a smile and a
Carefree attitude
But secretly, I wonder what it would be like to lift the veil
And reveal these hidden inner machinations
To let people see the damage they do when they use
Me as a means to their own end

I can't help but wonder, though, if it's not my own fault
If I didn't offer so much so readily and without
Recompense
Would I even be in this position now?
Would I ever have to question everyone's intentions
And their heart's true motives?
If I believed in myself more, believed that I'm worthy of
More, would that make it so?
Am I my own worst enemy?
Would having a white knight make a difference if I
Don't believe that I'm worthy of having it?

Gabriel Mero

# PART TWO: THEATRICAL

# Ghost

You came from nowhere, sudden and unbidden
Saying all the right things and showing me you cared
I had just about given up hope that someone would
Want me

I kept my walls up, willing my head, not my heart,
To lead the way
But the more we were together, I could feel my
Defenses crumbling
Your loving words and caresses quelled the doubt that
Lingered within
I allowed myself to fall for you, truly, wholly fall for you
It seemed like after an eternity, life was going my way
I could finally have the one thing in life I wanted but
Had hitherto been denied
You were the missing piece amidst my plentiful Blessings
I learned the exaltation of holding you as we slept
And your taste, the benefits of our passionate intimacy

One day, you vanished without a trace
Like the fading fragments of a half-remembered dream
Your disappearance left behind a vacuous emptiness
Heavy, unrelenting, debilitating
A heart was broken, depression took a vice-like grip

I had done everything right; I was certain of that
So why, then, did you leave me?
Why in such an egregious manner?

Had our time together really meant so little to you?
Had I been nothing more than a temporary source
Of entertainment?
Was I just someone you were trying on before
Deciding?

I had never known pain like losing you, had never
Questioned my worth so much
I tried to be patient, to give you time to miss me
But in this time of vacillation, I met someone
He helped me see my worth, that what you did was
A representation of you, not of me
I still don't feel anger toward you; I wish you
No hardship
But I do fear that your ghost will haunt me forever
That you will be the standard by which I hold
All other lovers
You were my first love, but I hate that you'll always hold
A special place in my heart
Your actions have proved that you are not worthy
Of that honor
I was the best partner you will ever have; I know that
Few others can stomach your narcissism and constant
Need for attention
I'm so afraid that you took my ability to love with you
My ability to love as purely as I did you
Will I ever be able to trust anyone to that extent again?
Will every affair be tinged with ephemeral vestiges
Of you?
Will I ever be able to let my walls down completely?
Or will I have learned it's best to keep parts of me
Closed off?

Gabriel Mero

I could drive myself mad questioning all of this
For you've certainly made me doubt myself even more
I know now I'll never get closure; I've resigned myself
To that
My only hope is that someday down the line
I'll be able to think of you and be able to miss you
But also be able to totally appreciate the time we
Spent together
Without the hindrance of remembering the pain
And it's after effects

# I Miss

I miss the feeling of your hand in mine,
Your head on my chest
I miss the comfort of knowing you were there,
That you chose me
I miss your "good mornings" and asking about my day
I miss your embrace and our goodbye kisses
I miss the sense of security you gave me
I miss that newfound contentment
I miss being a stranger to true heartbreak
I miss the last remaining innocence that you took
When you left
Your betrayal stung worse than the others because
I trusted you
Not only with my heart but also with my deepest
Fears and insecurities
I allowed you to go where no man had gone before
Believing that your words were true, your motives pure
Even after the pain, you put me through,
I still miss you

# Unanswered

Where does the love go when an affair ends?
Is it passed on to our next partner, or does it linger
Inside us
Like a ghost that can't cross over
Do we ever love the same way twice?
Or is each love new and different?
Can you ever truly stop loving someone?
Love is an enigma, a Rubix cube I have to understand,
Let alone solve

Even after all these years, there are still a
Plethora of unanswered questions, postulates, and
Hypotheses
Each lovers' touch has changed me in a
Microscopic way
Their kiss altering my genetic makeup
I am comprised of lovers, both past and future
Am I defined, then, by them? Or are they only a small
Part of who I am?
Am I nothing without these partners? Or are they simply
Speed bumps along the road of life?

# The Rules of Dating

The rules of dating are apparently quite simple:
If you're going on dates and having sleepovers
Then you're dating, but wait, there's more
Dating is basically friends with benefits
Just with a more intense attraction
Until you make it official, nothing matters
You are free to walk away at any time with no
Explanation or care
Once you're official, then you're actually
In a relationship
In a relationship, you apparently start to try in earnest
I say fuck the rules you cower behind
If you're dating, you're dating
Regardless of whether it's official or not
Stop making stupid rules to rationalize
Your own cold-heartedness and fear of commitment

Gabriel Mero

# Modern Age

I've never felt like I belonged to this time
Where technology has taken the place of
Human interaction
Where connection is relative and your next lover
Is merely a swipe or flirty message away
Attachments aren't formed as strongly now because
There are more available options now
Than there were before
I long for the simple days when meetings were
Face-to-face
When lovers had to write letters to stay in touch
And there was more respect for one another
A vital link has been detrimentally severed

# Narcissist Boy

Losing you felt like I couldn't breathe
I couldn't fathom facing the reality that I'd never
See you again
I couldn't bear the thought of going on without you
I blamed myself, assumed that I had done
Something wrong
I'd have done anything to get you back,
To hear your voice once more

As time has gone on, I've come to my senses
I realize now that I did absolutely nothing wrong
I gave you everything I had, treated you like gold
I thought you were perfect, a diamond in the rough
My feelings for you blinded me to your narcissism
To your codependency and immaturity
You always bragged about how good a person
You are
A good person doesn't ghost someone
After three months
Doesn't pretend like a whole relationship
Never happened
So you don't have to face the guilt of the hurt
You've inflicted

I hope you grow up one day and spiritually evolve
That you realize your own toxicity and stop
Playing the victim
I'm glad I got out of our affair with what few scars I did
You're not capable of loving anyone as much as

You love yourself
I pity anyone who gets tangled in your web of deceit
Anyone who believes your pretty words and temporary
Affections
I hope you enjoy keeping your own company
Because it's all you're ever going to have
If you can't learn to be more self-aware and have
Empathy for those you encounter

# Quondam Paramour

You were the culmination of fifteen years of
Fantasizing, of holding out for someone special
There were too many coincidences for
Our meeting not to be fate
We were on the same page in what we wanted
What our definition of a good, healthy relationship is
At long last, everything seemed to make sense
The final piece of this puzzle called life snapped
Into place
You made me feel sexy, intelligent, relevant
You nurtured the wounded survivor within
And brought me from the darkness and into the
Dazzling sun
That seemed to emanate from your mere being

It tormented me to learn of the ways
You'd been lacerated in the past
I vowed to treat you like the gold you are
You loudly broadcast your innate kindness,
Made me lower my guard and let you in
Holding you all night was paradise achieved
Kissing you was exaltation, my true Nirvana

I wish I'd seen your true nature before it was too late
Before I gave my heart and soul to you
Blind to your narcissism and immaturity
It wasn't until you ruthlessly cut me loose
Without a warning or any closure
That I finally noticed the well-concealed prurience

Gabriel Mero

Deeply rooted in you; I'd taken your words
At face value, believing your deception
I realize now that the fault lies
Not with me, but within you

I deserve someone who can love me unfettered
Who won't bring the ghosts of past liaisons
Into our interrelation
Who, while learning from bygone encounters
Is mature enough to start each new connection
With a clean slate
If you spend the whole time
Waiting for everything to fall apart
It inevitably will; that is no way to love

Affairs of the heart should be conducted
Freely, unhampered by the past, and lacking fear of
Anguish and betrayal
It should be passionate, and reckless, and wild
It should be a force more powerful than apprehension
And the obstacles that stand in the way

I know now that you are not ready for true love
That you lack the depth to be so free
That you haven't found your necessary independence
I could ruminate forever on why you did it
But it would only serve to keep the cuts open
I've reconciled myself with never getting a real answer
Your pitiful ending of our affair does not
Retract from what we had, of the experiences we
Shared

My only wish is that you someday become
The Saint you masquerade as
That you one day learn the meaning of
True love and that he treats you like a prince
That he reveres you, and cherishes you as I did

I miss your kiss, falling asleep with your head on my
chest
I miss knowing that at last someone saw the good
In me
And stayed by choice, not obligation
Though I'm loathed to admit it, I also hope that
Occasionally, if not frequently, I cross your mind
And you too, will reminisce about our time together

Gabriel Mero

# *Stay*

I am not ready to concede
Won't give up that easily
I refuse to believe that romance is dead
That love is nothing but a temporary feeling
I don't expect an unrealistic fairytale
Don't want to have a perfect love
I want to love a flawed person
And have them love my imperfect self
I want us to work together to build a shared life
I want someone who will love me enough to stay

# Please Be

Please be altruistic, have a heart of gold
Please be spiritual and on the path to Enlightenment
Please be mature enough to know my need for space
Isn't personal
Please be open-hearted and emotionally available
Please be sober, not reliant on drugs and alcohol
To cope
Please be understanding that I will always love
My cats the most
Please be clean; having good hygiene is so important
Please be patient when I throw up my walls and
Emotionally withdraw
Please be cool about my anxiety and hermit ways
Please be respectful of my strong opinions and views
Please be there for me when everything gets dark
Please be in possession of a great sense of humor
Please be motivated and willing to do your share
Please be tolerant of my anxieties and neuroses;
I promise I'm worth it
Please be good to me; if you are, there's nothing
I wouldn't do for you

Gabriel Mero

# Chinese Remedy

---

I have found that when I'm feeling down
Weighted down with immeasurable grief
I have an overwhelming craving for Chinese food
Something about the tang of soy sauce-laden rice
The crunch of sweet and sour chicken
And the grease of the egg rolls
Somehow quells the storm inside of me
In a way that nothing else can
At least nothing I can easily have at my disposal

# Best Friend

I've had many friends over the course of my life
Several people with whom I've become close
But until I met you, I had not been blessed
With a true friend that will defend me to her last breath
Who would fight all of my enemies just to keep me safe
Someone who not only sees my worth, but
Loudly proclaims it

You are the best friend that I've found
The Meredith to my Cristina; the Kirk to my Spock
I'm so grateful that I found you, that we have
Each other

Neither of us will have to wander in the cold alone
Whatever life may bring, nothing will tear us apart
Life is so much easier and less scary knowing I have you
Thank you for choosing me and for staying when
So many have fled

Gabriel Mero

# The Corner

In the corner where the camera can't see
Fingers fumble with belts and zippers
As eyes meet and breaths hitch
Lips are chewed, longing to meet
Pulses quicken, and lust takes the helm
This forbidden moment stretches an eternity
Forming an intense emotional connection
Past lovers are forgotten as old wounds heal over
Thought ceases, the caresses grow more intimate
Does this have to end?

# Amorous

My mind constantly goes back to the first
Night that we were intimate
It's like part of me is paralyzed there
Unable to progress even an hour later
I can still feel your warm hands exploring my body
Your mouth giving me pleasure as I caressed your head
The heat of our passion still blazes through
My synapses
Quickening my pulse and awakening my body
I wish I'd been ready for that night instead
Of weighted down with being newly single
I'd love to have kissed you and share that
Holy closeness, I've allowed so few to share

# Six Months

It's been six months since you silently
Slipped out of my life like a thief in the night
The first month was hell; misery incarnate
I couldn't understand how you could abandon me
As if I was of absolutely no consequence to you
Like the time we had spent together meant nothing
As time went on, the pain lessened, and I began
To see the world in bright hues again
I see now that we never would have lasted
I'd rather be alone than be unhappy with you
I don't fail to acknowledge the strides you
Helped me make
But I refuse to let you be the one to break my spirit

# London Fog

Country music twangs away over the sound system
As water percolates through coffee brewers
The boy with the chocolate brown eyes
And black glasses
Offers London Fogs and chocolate chip cookies
The scent of coffee, tea, and baked goods wafts
Through the air
Making my stomach rumble and my mouth water
I could grow to like it here

Gabriel Mero

# Cracked Screen

The cracks in the phone screen are deep
Much like the ones in my heart
They whisper stories of first love and heartbreak
Of clandestine rendezvous with a long
Sought after partner
Of arguments with a mother and midnight
Venting sessions
Of car repair and hair appointments
And sleepless nights spent anxiously awaiting a text
Of plans for a revamped book in the works
It's funny how an inanimate object is so vital
That it's present for all of these occurrences
And despite its fragility, it is a possession
Prized most of all

# I Am Free

I've never admitted this to anyone
I've certainly never said it out loud
Yes, when you surreptitiously disappeared from my life
It rendered my heart into near-decimation
Left me gasping for air, half-dead
I'd never felt such pain, such abandonment
But under this cacophony, I felt something else, too
"Free," I thought with relief  "I'm free "
Free from constantly having to worry myself
Sick about how long it would be until you came
To your senses
Free from my innate need to always have to
Impress you
Free from living in the shadows of all of your exes
But most of all, free from the sense of insecurity you
Invoked within me
And from your narcissism and manipulation
I am free to heal and move on with my life
Free to find someone else who will actually love me

# I Believe

I truly believe that you never meant to hurt me
That you really did want us to work out
Doubt whispers in my ear like a lover that
You were just bored and craved attention
That the only reason you chose me is how terrible your
Other options were
But I strive to block out this negativity and give you the
Benefit of the doubt
Sure, you ended things as callously as possible, but
What we had was good
You showed your interest and commitment
Time and again
You told me you thoroughly enjoyed our time together
You made promises laden with a future together
I believe that somewhere along the way
You got scared
It doesn't excuse what you did, but I can understand it
I was scared, too, but instead of destroying your heart
I used it to motivate me to try harder, to let my
Guard down, to believe
I believe one day you'll regret it and long for
What we had

# *Fantasy*

---

Since the first day we met, you have been so good
To me
You've listened to every word, rushed in when I
Needed help
Nurtured me when I needed attention to flourish
Loving you has certainly been a positive experience
I've grown in ways I never thought possible
Become someone I didn't even know could exist
I can't help but wonder: how long can this last?
How long before the fantasy is shattered and reality
Sets in?

In the fantasy, your love for me knows no bounds
Our faults are minimized, managed with ease
Our connection is solid,  able to stand the test of time
Whatever fights we may have will be few and
Far between
Maybe it would better to keep you as my dream lover
To keep you as a fantasy so I won't have to be hurt or
Disappointed by you
I can dream that I'm always on your mind
Or that I ever even cross your mind
I can believe that your generous acts are done
Out of love for me instead of pity or your innate
Kindness
I can feel special and loved in the small part of
Your heart

Gabriel Mero

Pretending that I actually inhabit more of your heart
than I actually do
Knowing you has been a blessed ride but the fantasy of
What could be
Is the epitome of a dream coming true

# Bring Me Back to Life

When, exactly, did it begin, this all-encompassing
Affection?
Was it the moment we first locked eyes? The tenth?
The twentieth?
Was it the instant the flirtation started, intense and
Invigorating?
Or the point when, having succumbed, our souls
As well as our bodies united?
It's strange, but lately, I can't seem to remember a time
When I wasn't crazy about you; when your attention
Didn't put me on cloud nine
Love has a way of paving over the pain of the past
And laying a path for a new, brighter, happier future
It wipes the slate clean and convinces us to try again
I'm so grateful that I met you, that you were the one to
Bring me back to life
I hope that I will never again have to feel the emptiness
Of my life without you in it

# Lagota

I believe that people come into our lives right
When we need them the most, when they can make
The biggest impact
You'd been on the outskirts for years, casual encounters
That always left me wondering what if?
But being shy, and lacking self-esteem, I never allowed
Myself to entertain the idea that you noticed me
Beyond the necessary
The summer was onerous, the pain
Unlike anything I'd ever felt before  First love always
Burns the deepest
I was desolate, my will to live gone like the boy
Who had stolen my heart and then vanished
Without a trace
Amidst this barren wasteland, along you came
There was a glint in your eyes, chemistry so intense it
Took my breath away
A friendship formed, a bond stronger than love
It seems you were brought to me at just the right time
Your presence has banished the pain from that
Heartache
Made me see that it is he, not I, who is the fool
You've become my rock, my confidant, my savior in
So many ways
Always there to save the day, to build me up
To illicit a beaming smile brighter than the sun itself
I know I drive you crazy sometimes, that I perhaps
Rely on you too much
But in the short time, we've really known each other

You have come to mean so much to me
I've let you inside my heart, lowered my defenses
You see the parts of me I hide from most everyone else
But you don't bat an eye; you accept them as
Part of me
And offer unwavering support
There are very few people
With whom I feel totally at ease, like everything will
Always be okay
Of all the blessings that the universe has
Bestowed upon me, you are undoubtedly the greatest
My hope is that I offer some of the same to you
My Lagota, who has been hurt and let down
Far too often
I know that nothing lasts forever, that we must enjoy
Our blessings while we have them, but my one prayer
One hope, is that you will be the exception to the rule
That I will never again have to face the dark and cold
Without you  I've grown so accustomed to our
Closeness, that the thought of losing it, of losing you
Makes my heart ache, leaves a foul taste in my mouth
I don't love freely, but I do love deeply
As long as you'll have me, I will be by your side

# My Dreams

I thrive in the night, for when I drift off to sleep
And my subconscious takes over
When I dream, I get to be with you
Unfettered by the constraints of our real lives
Anything is possible, nothing is off-limits
In my dreams, my hopes come to fruition
In my dreams, the love I feel for you is returned

# Red

Whenever I think of you, the color red comes to mind
Vibrant, warm, exuding élan
You stand out like a beacon among others of your kind
Effortlessly endearing, like your beloved Pokémon
Red is bold, striking, the personification of love
These are just a few of the qualities you share
A pleasant desideratum, like a winter-time glove
Unencumbered, you relentlessly show how much
You care
Your crimson touch ignites a conflagration in my heart
Sudden, but far deeper than any I've previously known
Our bond, remunerative, each doing their part
Both reveling in the unconditional love the other
Has shown
You're seared onto my heart, brilliantly scarlet
Claiming more of me with each passing day
The tranquility I've found in you is paradise incarnate
Our souls are inexorably tied in every possible way

# *Before/After*

Before you, my life was lackluster, void of color
After you, everything is vibrant and warm
Before you, the pain was overwhelming,
All encompassing
After you, the agony has been acknowledged
And released
Before you, I thought I'd die without being known
After you, I have been recognized and revered
Before you, all I'd known was solitude
After you, I have no fear of ever being alone
Before you, cold lingered infinitely
After you, the warmth has returned
Before you, I felt ugly and useless
After you, I've discovered my value
Before you, there was no one to listen
After you, I am heard and understood
Before you, I never thought I could do better
After you, I'm content where I am
Before you, I'd learned to close off my heart
After you, I love freely, laden with serenity
Before you, I thought I needed to be rescued
After you, I realize I am enough

# *Reasons*

---

There are probably a million reasons why
You shouldn't date me
I'm moody and distant at times
I like space and am set in my ways
I'm used to having to depend solely on myself
But there are several reasons why
You should date me
I'm loyal to the extreme
The physical aspect isn't the most important part to me
I'm clingy to a degree, but I don't want our lives to
revolve around each other
I understand that I can never come first, and
I respect that
No matter how much you infuriate me
I find myself coming back to you time and again

# I Love

I love the way you throw your head back
When you laugh
The twinkle in your eyes when your gaze meets mine
I love the way you look out for me
It's a pleasant change
The way you put your arms around me when
I get too cold
I love the way you hover – whether intentional or not
The affectionate way you tell me to drive safe and
Watch out for deer
I love the way our flirting makes me feel – like
Anything is possible
The fact that you stay to help me even though
You could go home and relax
I love the way you listen when I talk—you hang
On every word
The unwavering support you offer as if it's nothing
Bust most of all, under the jokes and longing looks
I love you; I love you to the brim of my scarred heart

# Secret Smile

It can be something so simple as a hand on the
Small of my back
Or the intense eye contact held just a little too long
Sometimes it's our clandestine, secret smiles
And the way you always step in to save the day
Or the copious favors you happily commit
I've never felt this cared for before
So understood, so safe, so valued

I never thought I could feel anything like this again
That I could thrive in the attention of someone else
I worry too much that I'm overly loquacious and
Get on your nerves
That you'll come to your senses and see how
Imperfect I am
But then I catch your eye, and you smile that
captivating smile
And my heart melts, my anxieties disappear
In those precious moments, I can believe it's true
That you're here to stay, that I've earned a sacred
Place in your heart
That's when I'm happiest, in these blessed moments
When our connection is so intense, it leaves no doubt
That something good is burgeoning deep inside

Neither of us is perfect; there's no denying that
But we do the best with the hand we've been dealt
Two loving souls struggling to survive in this
Chaotic world, no strangers to pain

Gabriel Mero

Somehow we found each other at just the right time
Maybe we'll stay friends, maybe we'll become more,
I hope we do
Knowing I have you to care is enough to get me
Through each day

# Your Eyes

A wise man once said that eyes are the windows
To the soul
In my time on this Earth, I have found no evidence to
Contradict this
The first thing I notice about someone, especially
A person of interest, is their eyes
They're certainly the first thing I noticed about you
Your eyes are chocolate brown, but the light that
Emanates from them make them sometimes
Appear lighter
This illumination reveals the loving soul within
Your eyes whisper of gentleness, respect, offer
Unconditional love and support
All of these are things that I have craved my whole life
In your eyes, I found a reason to smile again,
To persevere
In your eyes, I found salvation, a new purpose
In your eyes, I found a love I'd never
Believed could exist
In your eyes, I found myself

Gabriel Mero

# Loving Lamentation

When you're gone, my world seems askew
I don't want to need you this much, but I do
Our days apart are tinged with memories
Of your smile, your gregarious laugh
My dreams are haunted by the possibilities
Of what we could be if we tried
It's as if you're this omnipresent force
Controlling my life like a puppeteer with strings
These minuscule machinations linger long after
You leave
My heart was healed by you; now it beats for you
Every fiber of my being longs for your touch
When we're reunited, it begins all over again

# *Special*

---

I live for the moments you lavish me with attention
When you single me out and make me feel special
The way you throw your head back laughing at
My jokes
And the glint that emanates from your eyes whenever
We talk
I'm grateful for the way you've welcomed me
Into your life
I know you've been through your fair share of
Pain and betrayal
But you've allowed me inside and nurtured me as well
You've healed my wounds, made me see my worth
You take my idiosyncrasies in stride, embracing
Each one

I can't imagine where I'd be now if not for you
I have become a whole new person because of you
I've let go of resentment and found a new inner peace
I've learned to look beyond the façade into
The person within
I never thought that I could ever love you
But you've been so good to me, brought out
The best in me
I've realized that the one I wanted all along was you
You're not perfect; you can be closed off and
Temperamental
But your good qualities far outweigh the flawed ones

You take care of me, always step in to save the day
You have provided stability I thought didn't exist
You have ignited a passion I had buried long ago
Now that I've found you, I can't imagine my life
Without you in it
How did I ever get by without you?
Why did I ever want to?
I believe that our souls were destined to connect
Being with you feels like I'm finally coming home
I used to think that love was talking all the time,
And going on dates, and having sleepovers
But now I see that isn't always the case
Sometimes love is the little moments in between
Where your person takes the time to
Make you feel special

# You

I don't ever want this to end, this euphoric rush
That overtakes my body whenever you're near
It's like an impossible high that I can only get from you
And I am totally addicted, hooked completely
It's not just the help you provide
Or the intimate way you include me in your life
It's also the fact that you noticed me in the first place
I'm not used to that; I've never stood out
Never tried to grab the spotlight
But being with you makes me feel like the
Star attraction, accomplished in the highest degree
I finally see what I've been missing all these years
It wasn't the attention or the companionship
It was you, plain and simple you
You are the blessing I've long-awaited
The reward for keeping the faith
Through you, I have blossomed like a
Lotus flower

In the light of the sun that is you

Gabriel Mero

# *Spring*

Loving you is like spring
The cold and loneliness are banished
After too long a winter
Barren white is chased off and replaced by vivid greens
Life begins anew as vitality is restored
Under your loving care
The daylight is brighter, longer, all-encompassing
The drought is over, my rivers running deeply
Fear and doubt retreat under your steady battalion
Hope is restored as past trauma is diminished
And I can't help but think that this might be it
The one great love that we are all destined for
How else could you make me feel this way?
How else would all of our pieces fit together
So perfectly?
I pray that this spring lasts forever

# Super Hero

When danger looms, and darkness shrouds the land
When I'm sick and unable to eat a thing
When my physical strength isn't enough for the job
When depression tightens its vice-like grip
When past abusers suddenly reappear
When I need a safe place to stash something vital
When I need lotion applied to those hard
To reach places
When I need someone to listen and take my side
There you are, like a figure in tights
A super hero straight from the comics
Deeply committed to saving the day and
Making sure I'm okay as best you can
I may be your Kryptonite
But you're the one who gets me through each day

# Grateful

---

"Drive safe and watch out for deer," you say,
"just because the hunters are gone doesn't mean the
Deer are "
This is meant as a display of affection, a simplistic way
Of expressing your love
Once upon a time, this wouldn't have been enough
For me
I'd have been desperate for some small scrap of a clue
As to your true feelings
Now I'm grateful to share even a fraction of your time
To occupy even a minuscule part of your heart
I know your life is fine as it is, that you're content with
Your lot
But I can't ignore the love I feel for you, won't give up
On the possibility of us
Some things are worth having patience
Until that day, I'll be grateful for the time you give
The smiles, and contact, and attention you donate
So freely
Regardless of what transpires, I'll always be grateful
For you

# *Invisible String*

Like a single strand of the Fates' great loom
Some invisible string ties us together
Our connection goes back a generation
And continues with you returning home

Our families have been friends for years
Which lends credence to our destined meeting
We both came and went at different times
Narrowly missing each other until now

Some things can only happen when the timing
Is perfectly right
I truly believe that we are written in the stars
The universe was just waiting to bring us together
Until we both needed it most

Gabriel Mero

# *Empathy*

Being highly sensitive to others' emotions is no
Walk in the park
Sometimes you don't know if the feelings you're
Experiencing
Are yours or those of someone else
The affection you rouse within me is magnified
Because I know you care very deeply for me
I am no longer isolated in my experiences, trapped in
Solitary confinement
You're able to see inside me and recognize
The real me underneath the deficiencies
You see every nook and cranny of my being, yet you're
Still here

Somehow, you see something worth caring for in this
Decomposing figure
Something worth sharing your own scars with
You are the first person to see all of the ugliness
And remain to
Try to reassemble me into some semblance of a person
Your empathy has reinvigorated my soul, given me a
Fresh perspective on life
My value is reflected in your eyes, but manifested
Your empathy saved my life

# Two Become One

In the tapestry of my life, a mosaic of you
Occupies the most space
I remember the day we met as the day my life
First began
As the moment when my life changed irrevocably
Now everything is tinged with the essence of you
I see you in the crystalline snowfall
And the luminous rays of the sun
Even my dreams are haunted by possible
Futures with you
You have become the air I breathe
The blood that flows through my veins
With each heartbeat
You are the weight that keeps me grounded
The clarity amidst the haze of uncertainty
I know that everything will be okay as long as
I have you
If you were to ever fade from my life
An eternal winter would descend upon me
The sun would no longer shine, flowers
Would no longer bloom
But traces of you would remain,
Refusing to let me forget
How good I had it when you were by my side
The one constant in a life of tempestuousness

Gabriel Mero

# Vows

I never thought this day would come
That I would find someone who could love me for me
That someone would choose to stay by my side
That someone would push through my walls and see
Something worth loving

As I stand here with you now, I still can't believe
This is real
You were on the periphery for so long, vague and
Mysterious
I wanted to talk to you but was afraid you'd turn me
Down
Imagine my surprise then, when we finally met
And you told me you'd been watching me for years,
Longing for me
It's funny how life works sometimes
If we'd met an hour sooner, a day sooner, a week,
A month, a year
How different would our lives be now?
Would we still be together? Would we still be here?
Or would we have wrecked it, more scars that never
Healed?

I could spend the rest of my life wondering what if?
Or I could accept the gift of what we have
And dedicate the rest of my minutes to making you
Smile

Telling you how much you are loved
I'm so blessed to have you, and while I can't promise
To love you forever, I can promise to love you
As much and as long as you will allow

Thank you for loving me and for making me see
My worth
I hope we get forever, I really do
Because as far as I'm concerned,
No one could compare to you

# *Daylight*

This existence was empty and cruel before you
Devoid of warmth, color, and direction
Love was a fragment of a fractured dream
An unrealistic longing that couldn't be abated
Hope was a frail string I held on to
Dangling high above a treacherous pit of despair
One day you came into my life
And the Earth shifted on its axis
Order and balance were restored
Everything is brand new, as if
I'm seeing it for the first time
Hurt and isolation once defined me
Their scars readily available for all to see
Now every hurt is justified, rectified
Every wound healed shut
I used to cry because I felt alone
And now I cry because I'm so damned grateful
Grateful that I found you
That we found each other
After so long in the darkest night
I can finally walk in the golden daylight

# Precious Illusions

I believe that we all carry around these romanticized
Visions of what our lives will be like
Some long for the fairytale, while others settle for reality
Nothing is perfect, no one without flaw
Does The One really exist?
Or is this a construct force-fed to us as children
To perpetuate the tradition of settling down and
Getting married?
Is there truly only one person out there with whom
We're meant to live our lives?
Or is there an infinite number of potential partners?
I have had to learn to let go of some of these
Precious illusions
I had to accept that only I can rescue myself
If I can learn to truly love myself, then I can be open to
Loving another wholly
Holding others to the standards we hold ourselves to
Will inevitably lead only to hurt and disappointment
A relationship is two imperfect people coming together
To build something remarkable
Sometimes it has staying power; other times,
It fizzles out
But just because something ends doesn't mean
It wasn't special

Nothing lasts forever, as much as we wish that it did
Maybe in order to find true happiness, we need to
Reconcile our projections with reality and learn
To accept okay instead of demand perfection

Affairs of the heart are far more complicated than
Fairytales make them out to be; they're more complex
Unless you're willing to accept the flaws and
Take others as they really are, you're bound to be
Let down
Sometimes showing you care can mean more than
Saying it
If you're lucky enough to find someone who
Does their best to take care of your needs
Cherish them, care for them, nourish them
Because that is what love really is

# *Real Love*

Real love isn't getting along every second of every day
Or being in constant contact with one another
It's not discovering each other's body
Or always making your feelings apparent
Real love is supporting each other when
No one else will
And tender lines from genuine smiles
It's the joy you feel seeing your partner happy
And the little, seemingly unimportant moments
That add up to something bigger, something better
Real love is being strong enough to withstand
The storms
And fortify each other to become indestructible

# Beautiful Flaws

I don't need you to show me how you feel every day
Through big romantic gestures
I don't need moonlit serenades and
You always putting my needs before yours
I don't need expensive trinkets or
My own personal superhero
I don't need you to change who you are
To suit me—you're great as you are
In fact, I don't need anything from you
This is not to say I don't care
I do care very much; I want you very much
I want a long life with you that isn't filled
Every second with perfect happiness
But with the commitment to fight through
The hard times and come out stronger
I want to be your last first kiss
The first thing you see when you wake
I want you and all of your beautiful flaws

# *Receive*

They say that it's better to give than to receive
I've always tried to live by that idea
However, I haven't done it in a healthy way
I've perpetually felt that I have to buy peoples' love
That the only way to secure their affection is through
Constantly giving
Time, money, energy, kind words; I give them all freely
Each time, it has inevitably left me exhausted, broke,
and despondent
It wasn't until I met you that I learned a new way to live
Through your generosity and loving care
I have learned how to receive, how to love myself
Enough to believe I'm worthy of such genuine affection
If I can't believe that you love me for me
Then it isn't a healthy relationship, not worth my time

Gabriel Mero

# *Emotions*

My emotions hold dominion over me, I can't deny that
My hypersensitivity and empathy war in my
Subconscious
As hard as I try to be content with myself, I long for a
Soul mate
Someone who will not be my other half, but a separate
Entity desiring to enrich my life
But who is strong enough to stomach my desperate,
Constant need for reassurance?
Why does one bad day negate all of the good ones?
One unwanted word, and I'm questioning if you
Ever even cared
Is this how normal people live? Or am I entirely
Incapable of any semblance of normality?
It's as if I exist on a frequency much different than
What others do
I feel everything differently, far deeper it seems
Logic is useless once my feelings take the reigns
I cannot make myself see reason, no matter
How hard I try
I want to be as low-maintenance as possible
I know it's off-putting to be needy and demanding
But I can't quell the maelstrom inside

# *Complete*

I don't want you to be my other half
As if I'm somehow incomplete without you
I got over that romantic notion years ago
Decided to forgo such unhealthy codependent ideas
I as a person am whole—with or without you
You don't complete me; you complement me
You are a seasoning that adds to my flavor
A mirror that shows off my best angles
You bring out the best in me, bolster my
Self-confidence
You make my life better in every way
I never could have fully appreciated you
Without time on my own to forge my independence
And could not have learned how to be whole
Within myself

Gabriel Mero

# Good

I will never be Chosen like Buffy
Nor Charmed like Prue, Piper, Phoebe, or Paige
Never be a badass like Xena
Or a web-slinging superhero like Peter Parker
There is no radioactive spider waiting to bite me and
Make me extraordinary
No super witch powers to fulfill me
No destiny to give me a sense of purpose
No horrible past to spur me on to become a hero
All I have is an overwhelming need to be seen as good
To be seen as rational, and mature, and kind
In essence: to be seen as perfect
This unhealthy obsession has long ruled me
Despite knowing it is unrealistic
But some desires know no reason

# Let Me Be Brave

Four words have gotten me through scary, tough times
When I look out my window and see a blanket of snow
Covering the road –
Let me be brave
When I feel myself falling for a guy –
Let me be brave
When I have to tell my friend that I want him as
My lover –
Let me be brave
When I have to make an adult decision –
Let me be brave
When I post a new piece online, knowing
I'll face scrutiny –
Let me be brave
When I realize that one day I'll be alone and won't
Have an older family member to fall back on –
Let me be brave
These four words reverberate in my brain,
Echo in my ears, course through my veins
Bravery does not come easily to me,
But with enough prodding, it does come
Like Clara Oswald, before me,
I will face the raven
I will be brave

Gabriel Mero

# Red Converse

A red pair of Converse lies haphazardly on a
Bottom shelf
They're coated in a fine layer of dust, long neglected
They are the remnant of some long-ago fad
A must-have until something cooler came along
If they could talk, they would tell what they've seen
Meeting a handful of celebrities at Comic Con
Routine trips to the grocery store with your
Grandmother
Factories and transatlantic flights
Perhaps down the road, they will get a second chance
Get to have their day in the sun
Get to wear with use, a life well-lived

# What I Leave Behind

It's never too early to ponder your legacy
To ruminate on how you want to be memorialized
I want to be remembered as a generous person with
A kind heart
As someone who was able to survive the trials
I was subjected to
I want to be thought of as a person with a great
Sense of humor
Someone who was loyal to a fault and
Was always honest and reliable
My biggest hope is that one day, when I'm gone
People will remember me
That I will somehow have managed to make
Enough of an impact in others' lives
To be worthy of such reverence
This is what I leave behind

Gabriel Mero

# I Am

I don't know why so many treat me with disrespect
As if I exist solely to meet their needs
I am so much more than the money I can give
More than the favors I can do for you
Not just a body made to give pleasure
I'm not a genius, but my intelligence is not lacking
I'm no comedian, but I am entertaining
I am open-hearted, emotionally available
Empathetic in the highest degree

There are so many wonderful things about me
That get overlooked in lieu of instant gratification
I am capable of so many things
If only someone would give me a chance
I'm mature enough to not expect perfection
And to overlook understandable flaws
I am on an emotional journey to do better, to be better
Even though I'm sufficient as I am
I long for the day I'll be strong enough
To not be hurt when my worth isn't seen
The day when I will stop compromising my ideals
In order for someone to want to be with me

# Happy

If you had asked me at five
What I wanted to be
I'd have happily and quickly replied, "a scarecrow "
I've always loved Halloween and the idea of
Getting to wear a creepy mask and scare birds
Thrilled me more than words but embarrassed my mom
To no end

If you had asked at fifteen
What I wanted to be
I'd have nervously and slowly replied, "an actor "
I enjoy memorizing lines and doing my best to
Captivate someone with words and emotions alone
I can cry on command, a useful skill

If you had asked me at twenty-five
What I wanted to be
I'd have sighed with resignation and replied, "happy "
I'm sad to say that I am still striving for this seemingly
impossible goal which forever eludes me
But I won't give up hope

Perhaps if you ask me at thirty-five
What I want to be
I'll be able to smile and steadfastly reply,
"I'm perfectly happy where I'm at "

Gabriel Mero

# Little Me

If I could somehow commune with my younger self
There are so many lessons, and words of wisdom
I'd impart
Anything to prepare him for the road ahead
The trials and tribulations he will one day face
Little me, listen up, what I'm about to say is vital to your
Survival

Never stop loving with every fiber of your being
It's perfectly okay to give your all to something,
Especially love
Don't let your anxiety get the better of you
Nothing is ever as bad as you imagine it will be
Don't use up all of your energy so quickly
One day, far too soon, you'll long for the seemingly
Endless reserves you have
Don't be afraid to be yourself, anyone who can't
Accept you as you are
Is not worth worrying about

You are amazing as you are
Enjoy your carefree days while you can; revel in them
Being an adult is stressful, and you'll long for the days
When you had no responsibilities
Don't use material possessions to fill the void
You feel inside
Things are nice, but nothing can make up for what
You're missing

Don't be afraid to ask for help; we all need a little hand
Now and then
If we don't aid each other along the way
Life will be incredibly lonely

It's going to take a while, but you will meet people who
Understand you
They will make up for all of the betrayals and
Disappointments
Rely on the people you trust, but don't let it
Consume you
If you can't stand on your own two feet, you're
Doomed

Loyalty is never wrong; never regret the kindness and
Devotion you show to people, even when they hurt you
In response
You are going to face pain, sometimes so strong you'll
Want to die
But always remember that the storms come just before
The sun
Everything gets better if you want it to, if you try
Don't be afraid of hard work, you won't get anywhere
Without it
And there is nothing admirable about being lazy

I wish I could skip the bad stuff and focus solely on the
Good
But the bumps along the road are part of what will
Inevitably
Shape you into the warrior you're destined to become

Gabriel Mero

A survivor reliant not on physical strength and prowess
But your ability to overcome it all and still retain
Your kind spirit and loving heart
Never lose that; those two things are your greatest
Assets
Hone your sense of humor, and you'll have three
Wonderful attributes
By which to define yourself, to set you apart

And lastly, also importantly, be kind to yourself
Don't beat yourself up for your mistakes,
Learn from them
Allow them to push you to do better, to be better
And never, never, let go of the light you hold inside
That light will brighten up the darkness of
Someone special
Together you'll want for nothing; you'll have all you
Need

# *Call Me*

You can call me a witch because I believe in
Magic and the power of the Earth

You can call me a Buddhist because I believe in
Meditation and the sanctity of all life

You can call me a Hindu because I believe in
Reincarnation and the immortality of the soul

You can call me a Christian because I believe in
God and the principles of the Bible

You can call me a spiritualist because I believe in
Treating others as I would want to be treated
And that we control our own happiness

You can call me what ever you need to make yourself
Comfortable

Gabriel Mero

# Feminine Energy

I have never felt like much of a man
All my life, I've gravitated toward feminine things
Dress up, musicals, female singers, and
Female-led shows
Nine times out of ten, I relate to a woman character
Not because I think of myself as a girl
But because I feel a strong connection to the
Female spirit
I can relate to its sense of oppression and struggle
Of not being seen for my worth and deemed weak
In recent days I have dipped my toes
Into the masculine world
And found that while on the whole, it's not my
Cup of tea
I can straddle the line perfectly, a resident of
Both realms
I am a man that has been graced with the
Best of both worlds:
The body of and temperament of a man bearing
The energy and emotional maturity of a woman
I bask in that feminine energy like a flower in sunlight
I am no longer ashamed but empowered

# *Unsinkable*

---

Life has not always been kind to me
I'm not sure it's some karmic retribution for
A slew of transgressions carelessly committed
In a past life
A fray in the Fates' great loom
Or a method of forging me into a tougher being
But despite what is thrown my way, I refuse to
Let hate win, to kill the kindness that abundantly
Grows in my heart
I refuse to douse the light that shines so deeply within
I refuse to let the darkness win and claim my
Immortal soul
I am unsinkable

# *Thirty*

---

For as long as I can remember, I have feared thirty
Saw it as the literal end of my precious youth
In your twenties, you can still make mistakes, tumble,
And fall
But in your thirties, you're expected to have it sorted
People no longer justify your faults; excuse your
Missteps

The security blanket has been torn away
At thirty, I have not reached where I always thought
I would
I have not achieved total independence
I still have unresolved issues, unconquered fears
I'm not rich, not overly educated
I have dreams still unrealized and unfulfilled
But I have a maturity and wisdom lacking
In so many others

Integrity and morality in abundance
I have everything I need
And maybe that's enough

# 2021 Meditation

The meditation for 2021 is to smile more
To be more grateful for the blessings I do have
Instead of focusing on what I cannot possess
To be stronger not just physically but mentally
To let others' cruelty run off of me like water
Off a duck's back
To be more independent 'til I don't have to rely on
Anyone but myself
To love myself when others cannot
To stand up for myself regardless of the consequences
But most importantly, to stop letting fear and anxiety
Hold dominion over me to the point of
Allowing myself to grow stagnant

Gabriel Mero

# *Affirmations*

It's not rude to not allow others to walk all over you
It doesn't make you conceited to acknowledge
Your worth
It's not narcissistic of you to love yourself
It's not pompous of you to know your intelligence
It's not reckless to take chances
It's not foolish to let someone into your heart despite
Being hurt in the past
You're not lazy for sleeping past noon
It's not selfish to take time for yourself
It's not a sin to masturbate and explore pleasure
It's not healthy to eat only once a day
It's not bad to have meat on your bones
It's not self-indulgent to meditate
It's not egocentric to pray for yourself
It's not unbecoming to have emotions
It's not weak of you to care

# *Corona Pandemic*

If you do test positive for this virus
Then chances are that I have it too
I've always felt that this pandemic was unstoppable
That there was no way that any one of us would go
Unscathed
No matter what happens next, I just want you to know
That I don't blame you at all
I know that you would never intentionally hurt anyone,
Let alone me
My greatest fear in all of this is that something bad
Will happen, and you'll never forgive yourself
You deserve better than that cross to bear

Gabriel Mero

# Carrie Fisher

As a child, you were a spunky space princess
Who didn't need to be rescued and led the Resistance
I admired your quick wit and bravery
But had no idea of the true woman behind the icon
As I grew up, I came to see that the attributes I
Thought belonged to Leia actually were yours
But you had so much more to give
Despite your demons, your sense of humor was
Razor sharp and ever-present
Your survivor spirit saw you through several dark days
But your spirit remained kind, an imp in human form
You never held your tongue, not when the truth
Needed out
The day we lost you, I cried like a baby
I felt like my hero was gone, and I could never be
Strong again
But then I realized that in loving you, I had adopted
Your attitude
Your strength became mine, shared
I'm grateful to have lived at the same time as you
And I want you to know that as much as I love Leia
I will always, always love Carrie more

# Guardian

For many, having kids is their raison d'être,
Their life's dream
And I never understood why; surely there are  more
Fulfilling paths in life
It wasn't until I stepped in as your guardian
That I firmly grasped the concept of parenthood
Oftentimes, you drive me up the wall to no end
You don't give me space; you follow me like a dog
Sometimes I have to self-medicate to keep from
Losing my cool
But there is an odd sense of delectation that
Comes with it
For too long, I've looked for meaning and rapture in
the arms of a lover
I never imagined I could be found in caring for a
Neglected child
Perhaps it's selfish to need to be needed
I'm doing my best to set a good example and see that
your needs are met
In caring for you, I've found a contentment that 'til
Now, has evaded me

Gabriel Mero

# *Khaleesi*

You were supposed to be the perfect cat,
My one true companion
After all, you chose me, not the other way around
For a while things were great, but you started to
Pull away
I was furious when you got pregnant, but I knew
Something good was coming
You birthed five kittens; I was there for it all, holding our
Paw and offering encouragement
After you got fixed, you cooled toward me, not even
Letting me pet you but for the rare occasions
Now, you're often seen in my Grandma's bed, offering
Her solace
I'm not envious of your other affections, just grateful
When I receive them
It's funny how things work out, sometimes not as
Planned
I kept two of your babies, one of which has more than
Fulfilled your role
Without you, I'd never have gotten her, and that would
Be a tragedy
How ironic that you ended up to be the mother of my
Happiness
I'm eternally grateful for your contribution

# Alistair

My baby boy, my beautiful baba
You are my golden son, my only son
I might not be your biological father
But I was there when you were born and
Have spent the majority of your days with you
It's true that as a cat, you most likely won't live as long
As I'd like
That there will always be an untempered part
Of you that hard as I try, I cannot grasp
Regardless, I want you to know that you
And your sister have my enriched life in so many ways
You taught me patience and how to love
You comforted me when my world was obliterated
Your heart beats in mine eternally
We are one now and forever

# *Romana*

I never thought that I could ever love anything as much
As I love you
The minute you were born, an unbreakable bond
Was forged
Even as a kitten you, pulled at my heartstrings
With your big gold eyes and tiny head
I made you a promise then that I would
Care for you come what may
That I would protect you to my dying breath
That you would know every second how much
You are loved

People think it's silly because you're just a cat
They say that you only see me as the person who
Feeds you
But when my heart is breaking, you're the one
Giving me comfort; at night, it's you snuggled up
With me
I dread the day we'll have to say goodbye
Nothing in the world can prepare me for that dark day
In the four years we've been together, you've become
A vital part of me
Like oxygen to my lungs, blood to my veins
You have shown me unconditional love
And opened my heart in ways I never thought possible
The deep love I now have, I have because of you

You might just be a cat, but I love you like a
Best friend, like a daughter; there aren't words
For the depth of love I bear you; your paw prints
Have left an indelible mark on my heart, never to be
Erased
Of everything I've done, you are the one thing that I'm
Most proud of

Cats can be so fickle, but our love is deep and real
I wish that you could live forever, or at least long
Enough for us to go together, so neither of us would
Have to suffer the pain of living without the other

# Midnight Musings

I don't want this divide between us
It's confounding and unnatural
I'd like to share a comfortable familiarity with you
To be able to call you after a hard day and get
Sympathy and understanding, comfort and
Reassurance
I'm not convinced that will ever be in the cards for you
And me
I fear our meetings will be laden with awkwardness
And anxiety
I'd like better for us

# Mother Darling

You never wanted to become a mother, not because
You're a monster
But because you've always felt you would do a
Terrible job at it
That you would ruin the young life and carry the
Guilt with you forever like a badge of dishonor
I can't blame you; being a parent is scary, and it's a lot
Of sacrifice and responsibility
I want you to know, though, that you did just fine, you
Can forgive yourself your shortcomings
You weren't perfect, but none of us is
You did the best you could with what you had
I grew up to be an intelligent, witty, kindhearted person
So you gave me the fundamentals
I need to succeed in this life
My anxiety and lack of faith in myself isn't
Through any fault of yours; but of a random chemical
Imbalance inside my brain
I hate that you beat yourself up about my
Imperfections, they're just one small part of who I am
You fail to see all of the wonderful things that
I am because of you
We don't always see eye to eye, sometimes we fight,
But that doesn't mean that I don't love you
Or that I for one second wish my mother had been
Someone else
I've forgiven you for the mistakes you made while
Raising me; I think it's time that you do the same
You were there, which is more than some

People can say
You stood up for me against the bullies and
Crabby teachers
When I had an anxiety attack, you never pushed me or
Told me to get over it, even though you
Didn't understand it
You never discouraged me from seeing my dad, even
Though he only ever hurt and disappointed me
While you never understood my artistic, musical side,
You allowed me to embrace it
Your only concern about my sexuality was for
How hard of a life it is; otherwise, you've been
Supportive
So, don't ever for one second think that you've been
A bad mother or that you've ruined me for life
Despite your own faults, you were able to make
A good person, you should be proud of that

# Guardian Angel

I think I was five the first time we met
You seemed nice but were otherwise no different
From the others
I got along well with your two sons
We'd stay up late performing: me singing Patsy Cline
Your boys dancing, and you cheering me on
I wasn't used to that, that ready acceptance

Time went on and, you stuck around, you became
A vital part of our family, always there to talk
Or listen, a shoulder to cry on, strong arms to embrace
You didn't often get angry, and when you did, your
Words were never harsh, that too, was new to me
With you, I knew that I was in a safe space
That I could be myself free from judgment, from
Condemnation
Your heart shone brighter than any star in the night sky
Seeing you with your kids was to see pure pride and
Love
Everything about me that others criticized, you
Championed
A tough guy, you never shamed me when I cried
When I talked, you listened, not with the half ear of
Every other adult
But with your whole being, all your attention

Nothing was too dumb, nothing unachievable
With three boys of your own, you took me under
Your wing
And loved me just as you loved them
More than my dad, more than my step-dad,
Unconditionally

I took it for granted that you would always be there
I never told you that I loved you or thanked you for
All you did
You always put others before yourself, to a fault
Working hard to make sure the ones you loved were
Provided for
In the midst, you neglected to care for yourself

It's been almost ten years since you passed away
I never got to say goodbye, sure to the end that you
Would beat it
That you would be okay because you had to be
Because I needed you  Because so many people
Needed you
I hope you'd be proud of the man I am today
The lessons you taught me still reverberate in my soul
Kindness is free, so give it often and copiously
Love is the most powerful force on Earth; nothing can
Compare

Fear can be overcome with due diligence; you just
Have to try
Money is immaterial; it's your heart that counts
I carry these lessons with me each and every day
As I strive to be the best I can be
And although you aren't here anymore to share
A laugh or offer support
When I close my eyes and think of you, you're there,
In my heart

# Un-Natural Selection

Sometimes when a person dies, it is dismissed as
Natural selection
The archaic, detached belief that only
The strong survive
That no matter how hard you try to survive,
Some people are just genetically inferior

My Grandma Mary was the best woman
I've ever met
Kind-hearted, generous, not a drop of cruelty in her
She didn't live to be sixty; was this natural selection?

My uncle Tony – more like my dad – loved me
Like his own son
He cared about my well being, accepted me as I am
He didn't live to be fifty; was this natural selection?

I don't subscribe to such trite rationalizations
It seems that most times, it's the good ones that go
This un-natural selection sees no reason

# Roses for June Lois

All my life, you've been this monolithic figure
Strong, steadfast, invincible
You are the glue that has held this family together
Through all the fights and ended affairs
Whenever we needed a rock to lean upon
You've been there to make it all better
Offering to help as much as possible
You took each dilemma in your stride
Making it look so effortless, you made us believe that
We could too
Nothing could keep you down; nothing could
Break you

As kids, we loved to test your will and your patience
Reveling in making you mad enough to scream
Because we knew that at the end of the day
You'd love us, come Hell or high water

As the years have passed, you've gotten smaller
You move more slowly, you sleep a lot more
The strength that you've wielded so effortlessly
For decades, has begun to wane
This new, fragile you is hard to observe
Seeing how, as much as you fought, even you
Can't stop the hands of time
You've resigned yourself to your ultimate fate
And lost your unwavering control

Gabriel Mero

But if there's one thing you've taught us
It's that perseverance is not a choice, but a necessity
Anything can be overcome with an iron will

Someday, perhaps soon, perhaps not
You'll have gone on your final, great journey
And our hearts and lives will be monumentally less
But your memory will spur us all on to honor
Your spirit and fight to carry on, to be strong

I don't know how we'll carry on without you, for
You've seared yourself onto us eternally
But not even the coldest winter could stop our
Memories of you
And in the spring, when the flowers bloom, I'll plant
Roses for June Lois
A truly remarkable, incomparable woman

———————————————————————

---

# *PART THREE: DARK AND THEATRICAL*

---

# It's Okay to Be Sad

It's okay to be sad
For in these moments of melancholy
We get to experience our memories
In a new light, see them from a different angle
We get to appreciate things in a new way
Everything ends; nothing is eternal
Try as you might, you can't avoid despondency
It's better to embrace the inevitable
Rather than try to deny its eventual arrival
Just don't let the desolation overwhelm you

# *Thanksgiving 2020*

It boggles my mind that some families actually
Get along
Actually spend holidays together without contempt
And tension
Do normal families really exist? How do they do it?
I've secretly yearned for that tranquility my whole life
It must be nice to have an army of people to have
Your back
Allies that can never sever those ties
All I've known from my blood roots is treachery and
Betrayal
I wish that our collective wounds could be healed,
Our shattered family repaired
Of course, I know that this is merely a fantasy
A goal of the absolute highest unattainability
Yet, an infinitesimal part of me holds on
Longs for the bridge in our separation

Gabriel Mero

# Acceptance

Until tonight, I hadn't gone to that store or restaurant
Since the times that we went together
For me, these places are forever tinged with

The essence of you
Too long, I've avoided them, not wanting to
Rid myself of the final vestiges of our brief affair
But I realized that it wasn't you, holding me back
It was me  I was frozen in inaction by memories
Of a tryst that was beyond forgettable
I have to move on and stop giving you the power
To keep me in a rut of misery and despair
A self-imposed exile that gripped me tightly
I'm in a place now where I can forgive you for

The pain you inflicted
I can refuse to label you a bad seed because
Of one egregious deed
I've made peace with the knowledge that our story

Is done
And while there wasn't much there, in actuality
It was still a sacred experience for me
That led me to something so much better

# *Perfect*

---

If you're perfect, then people will love you
If you're perfect, no one will speak ill of you anymore
If you're perfect, you'll never be lonely again
If you're perfect, you can finally relax and accept the
Peace you deserve

You're exhausted from this endless pursuit
But who cares? Achieving perfection will be worth
Every sleepless night, every twinge of anxiety
Mask your imperfections, make yourself malleable
Like clay
So that you can be what everyone wants and
Needs you to be

If you're not perfect, then what good are you?
If you're not perfect, what use are you to anyone?
You're highly sensitive, neurotic, needy; nothing good
Until you rid yourself of these bad traits,
No one will ever want you
No one will ever love you or value your opinion
It's okay for others to err, but not you
You must be perfect

Gabriel Mero

# Anxiety

I envy those to whom anxiety is a stranger
Those who never have to overthink each action
Question each choice, every thought
That niggling voice is a cruel master
A ruthless slave driver bent on domination
It doesn't care that I hurt
That it is the leading cause of my debilitation

Oftentimes it feels like no one understands
No one gets that I don't want to be this way
I don't want to be weighed down by doubt
Drowned by my own overpowering neuroses
I am alone in my mental purgatory
With no sign of merciful reprieve
It's bleak, not having a sense of belonging
I am a solo nomad in my own life
Forever searching for that elusive thing called normal
My life has barely begun, and I'm already exhausted
Ready for an end to this misery
It's impossible to trust when you always get burned
Constantly get let down and abandoned
What I wouldn't give to live life like everyone else

# Neuroticism

I've always envied the self-assured type who
Never have to wonder
I'm always questioning, always trying to figure it all out
I've never been wanted; not by anyone,
Not anywhere; not for long
It's a lonely life when every relationship is dissected,
Examined from every angle
To try to find proof of its legitimacy and longevity
How long will it be until the desire fades from your eyes
And I'm discarded like yesterday's dirty clothes?
How long until my faults take the reigns and can no
Longer be easily dismissed or ignored?

I fear that I am doomed to wander this Earth desperate
To belong to someone, to be wanted
But to be forever cast aside, forever slightly out of
Reach from this most basic of human needs
More than anything, I yearn for the comfort of
Mattering to someone, to know I've affected them

At my core, I am a giver, striving to provide for
The people I love and be what they need
Not because I enjoy giving but because in my
Twisted mind, I believe that if I don't,
They won't love me

Gabriel Mero

I've been conditioned my whole life to believe that I
Am less, that I am inherently wrong
Perhaps it's foolish of me to place
Such a burden on another, but it's obvious that I will
Never be able to meet that need
For myself

I can be so strong for everyone else,
But when it comes to myself, I'm weak

# Insecurities

---

I wish that my mental health was up to par
That my insecurities didn't define who I am
I have never felt good enough
Not to be happy
Not to be loved
I feel like a burden to everyone
Like I'm an annoyance that must be tolerated
I feel ugly, and fat, and most of all, unworthy
Of all the wonderful things this life has to offer
Some nights I lie awake in bed and wonder
If I died, would anyone notice?
Would anyone even care?
I wish I was stronger and could silence these insecurities
I'm not
It's an albatross I wear daily

Gabriel Mero

# Reflections

The person I see reflected in the mirror
Is not a man with whom I am acquainted
I gaze upon him with the privileged detachment
Of a stranger, dissecting and cataloging each
Imperfection
The overly long nose, the droopy eyes
The barely concealed double chin
The one crooked tooth and high forehead
The livid patches of eczema marring my otherwise
Milky skin
Most of all, the saggy, bloated tummy
That never ceases to disenchant
I can bestow so much love on everyone else
Yet me, myself, I starve, waiting for
Someone to show me the unconditional
Love I've never experienced firsthand
This insalubrious trait a cancer
Masticating my self-esteem with each
Bite; mere bones persist, a remnant
From more jovial times  Can I truly
Love another until I've mastered
This exigent endeavor?
Can I believe that I'm worthy of such love
If I don't have a salient affection for myself?
Is it wrong to learn to love oneself
Through the act of loving another?
Is this perfect symbiosis?
Or a prelude to codependency?
Will I master this craft in time to

Savor my days, or will I languish
In purgatory, destined to be eternally dispirited?
Must all my opinions of myself be
Dependent upon the approval of others
Who view themselves with more benevolence than
That with which I gaze upon myself?
I have no answers; my only recourse is
The same hope that gets me through each day
The aspiration that I will one day love myself
Just as leniently as I love others here and now
That I may be blessed with an abundance of
Amorousness for all

# *Outside*

All my life, I've felt I existed on the outside
Inherently apart from the rest of society
Forever doomed to walk alone
Never understood, never belonging
The few who have attempted to bond
Have inevitably abandoned and betrayed me
More wounds I can add to my generous supply
Despite this crippling disappointment
I remain hopeful that one day
Someone will see me and will be able to
Accept me as I am, will appreciate my flaws
As much as my positive attributes
Who will give home a new meaning
And make me feel like I belong
Who will nurture the scared, wayward child
Within and help him blossom into a
Semblance of a happy, healthy being

# Written in the Stars

The hard truth is that no one will ever love me enough
To make up for the fact that I don't love myself
No one will ever love me enough to fight for me
Until I accept that only I can save myself
I am inexorably setting myself up
For inevitable disappointment
I will never be anyone's first choice
Never be the one to be chased
Never hold anyone's interest for long
For some reason, it's written in the stars
That my path must be walked alone
Forever an outsider

Gabriel Mero

# My Life As I See It

If my life were a movie, I'd want it to be a
Romantic comedy
With an earth-shattering love that nothing can
Tear asunder
And laughs so intense it leaves your sides aching
This would be preferable to the reality
If my life were actually a movie
It would be a depressing drama not unlike
*Les Misèrables*
But without the swelling musical numbers and
Compelling characters
It would be a sad story of a boy who never
Felt he belonged
Who wanted so badly to be accepted, to be loved
Whose only solace was a clowder of flea-ridden cats
Who are merely the victims of Stockholm Syndrome

# *Not Like the Movies*

If you sit around and wait for your life to play out
Like it does in the movies, then I'm sad to say
That you're going to be monumentally disappointed
There is no fairytale happily ever after in the cards
No knight in shining armor waiting to save you
Sometimes bad things happen to good people
And good things happen to bad people
Good doesn't always triumph; some dreams go
Unfulfilled
All you can do is hope for the best and appreciate
A good thing while you have it

Gabriel Mero

# Unfinished

My body is an abandoned mansion on a hill
Overlooked, neglected, a blurred image in
The background
I am not well-maintained; there's no one to
Do the upkeep
Within my walls lie memories – of happiness, sadness,
Anger, and betrayal
Ghosts wander around aimlessly, lost forever
In purgatory
We forsaken souls linger, yearning for absolution,
For acknowledgement
If anyone cares enough to tackle this fixer-upper
I could be shiny again, solid again, habitable again
I may be broken, no longer new and pristine
But I still have something beautiful to give

# *Greatest Fear*

I have a deep admiration for strong, independent spirits
Those have always been the souls that I have
Gravitated toward
Lately, I have come to the realization that all of
My heroes end up dying all alone
In their youth, they have wild, tempestuous love affairs
But for some reason are unable to maintain
A long-term relationship or healthy connection
Am I doomed to follow in these isolated footsteps
Or will I be able to break from the mold
And keep the spirits of my idols alive
While rectifying the mistakes they made?
My greatest fear is dying alone
Not having someone to even care that I'm gone

# Sometimes

Sometimes I think you tolerate me
Because you have to
That rather than setting me straight, you'd rather
Maintain the status quo

Sometimes I think you just pity me
That you see how lonely and beat down I am
So you show me basic decency

Sometimes I think you're just a friend
That you got over your crush on me after we were
Intimate
And the nice things you do are your way of
Assuaging your guilt

Sometimes I think you're still into me,
That our tryst strengthened it for both of us
But you're put off by the complications we face
So we stay in this limbo, vacillating between
Friends and more, leaving it unresolved

# *Renascence*

I was in the winter of my life when I met you
Barren, bleak, desolate, I was a facsimile of alive
Hope was lost, I was adrift, there was nothing I could do
It felt like the sun had perished; nothing could thrive
Your eyes on mine ignited a phlogiston fire inside,
Ignited a spark
Despite just meeting you, I felt as though I'd known you
All along
As if our souls were acquainted, illuminating the way
Out of the dark
I instantly knew something was beginning, I cut short
My swan song
Your kindness and generosity healed my wounds,
Brought about spring
Suddenly, the past no longer existed; you became my
New forever
Wizened body, resuscitated, my salubrious heart
On a string
Ours is a bond that nothing can ever tear asunder
I found heaven in your arms, your body my bliss
Everything became clear, each trauma efficacious
Now I live for your touch, drown in your eyes, thrive in
Your kiss
You took a dead husk and made it bloom, bright and
Ostentatious

Gabriel Mero

# *Father*

In my formative years, I worshipped the ground you
Walked upon
You hung the moon; no one could be cooler
Even though you weren't a regular cast member
In the play that was my life
There was no one that I loved more
I overlooked the unpleasant occurrences
Since they also brought the good ones
I'd have done anything to never have to leave
Your side

That all changed one day, I'm not sure when
I still overlooked your flaws
Your drinking, your inconsistent attention
But I couldn't fail to notice the lengths
That other dads went to see their kids
And it broke my heart to know that you didn't love me
Like that
I know losing my mother, and your mother, hit you hard
Watching your son being raised by another man
Had to be a deep wound to your pride
Especially since he gave me a "better"
Life than you could ever provide
The rest is entirely inexcusable

How I'd come to see you, and you'd stick with
Your plans
The infrequent phone calls our only connection
The selfishness you fail to acknowledge

More than a decade later, you've decided
You're ready
You're potentially offering something I'd have killed for
As a boy
Sadly, I've realized that it's too late, that fantasy
Is dead
The scars are too plentiful, the wounds too deep

I found a surrogate for the love I wanted from you
For a while, I had the dad I'd always longed for
I was devastated when he died,
But I'm grateful I had him
He was everything you could never be
He never hurt me; he supported me
He loved me unconditionally
And the most lamentable part is that
We weren't even related by blood
This man who came into my life at five
Could love me more than my own father

It's not that I hate you or hold any grudges
But I killed off the part of me that once needed you
I've learned to rely solely on myself
To cut off anything that is likely to bring pain
I feel nothing for you, nothing but irritation
That you had to realize too late that you wanted this
Where were you when I was proud to call you Dad?
Why did my "dad" pass away too young,
Instead of you?
Why do I feel guilty for brushing you off?
Why do I feel that you're owed something?
Is it true that one day you'll be gone, and I'll

Gabriel Mero

Regret my stance?
That I'll wish for a do-over, to fix our disconnection?
And when that day comes, when you've breathed
Your last
I can only hope that the pain you've inflicted
Won't be too much to revive that long-lost hero

# *Stepfather*

I can't remember a time in my life where I didn't
Know you
You came along when I was so young that
By the time I became sentient, you were
Already deeply rooted in my life
You were a usurper, an imposter of my dad
No matter what you did, you couldn't compete
I would never like you, let alone love you
As much as him

I don't know when it started, but you turned cold
Your words turned barbarous, your touch unpropitious
While I was still forming, at my most vulnerable
You planted the seeds of what would one day
Grow into a garden of self-loathing, of self-doubt
You made me feel like the bullies were right
That I was somehow less, that I didn't deserve
Happiness
You gave me things—books, toys, movies
But starved my faith in myself
You loathed the attributes that made me
Who I am, tried to mold me into
Your vision of who I should be

Then your son was born, and it became clear
From the reverent way that you doted on him
That the problem was that I'm not yours
I could never up to your perfect standards
Because I am tainted by DNA not passed on from you

Gabriel Mero

Why did you choose a woman with a kid?
How could you be so immature as to punish
Me for my attitude barely out of diapers?
For years I suffered the deeply-rooted trauma
Of your maltreatment, somehow still strove
To win your impossible approval

Eventually, I learned that I would never
Make you proud, that I shouldn't even try
I was running myself ragged to win the approval
Of someone who had rejoiced in beating me down
In controlling me to an unhealthy height
Instead of trying to make you proud
I realized that I should be focused on myself
That someone as pernicious as you should
Not decide my worth, should not dictate
My happiness and dismiss my accomplishments
That it is you, not I, who is not good enough
Your intelligence may be well above average
You may be more successful, have more status
But on a spiritual level, your soul is far lesser
Than mine  In terms of goodness, possessing a heart
I stand champion over you, and reign supreme

It's enough for me to know I'm a better person than you
That there are people I have encountered
Who think I'm extraordinary, who can love
Me for the person I am, who can't care
Unless I change my most vital parts
It hurts me to know that I can't forgive your
Transgressions

Not that you'll ever acknowledge them or seek
Exculpation
If Hell froze over and one day you did
I know in my heart I couldn't provide an acquittal
In your callousness, you took a helpless child
And annihilated his belief in his own meritoriousness
That act, repeated so often and so egregiously
Can never be forgotten or justified

# Little Brother

I never wanted you to be born
Being an only child suited me just fine
When Mom told me the news, I cried like a baby
Because somehow I implicitly knew that my time
In the limelight was coming to a close
That I would become the Other Child
And you would intrinsically overshadow me

Time went on, and we learned of your condition
I hated how much it hurt our mother, how it
Ultimately led to the end of the love between her
And your father
It's not your fault, of course
When I had to help take care of you is when my
Resentment for you festered
It wasn't fair that I had
To forgo honing my craft so that I could babysit you
You weren't my child, so how were you my problem?

Time has gone on, and I've matured immensely
I no longer harbor feelings of jealousy or contempt
More than anything, I feel tremendous guilt
Guilt that I was born "normal" while you were
Doomed to live a life in which you are trapped
Inside yourself
You had so much potential, of that I am certain
I may be better looking, but you're far more intelligent
More social, unhindered by anxiety and my
Smothering neuroticism

Gabriel Mero

You would have accomplished wonderful things
Far greater than anything I will ever accomplish
It doesn't seem fair that you, with so much promise
Were dealt this card when it could have so easily
Been me  Should have been me
If there was a way
I could make it right, swap places with you
I would, in a heartbeat, without hesitation
You were born to take this world by storm
Not like me, who was born to worry incessantly
And overthink each exchange
We were both accidents
But you were less so than I; I say this with no bitterness
I wish I could make it right and give you the life
You could have had
The life you deserve

# Nicotine

I rue the day I allowed you into my body
Like a bad lover
As a child, I swore that I'd never smoke
I knew full well the consequences,
The damage you inflict

On a warm spring day, I decided that trying one
Wouldn't kill me, wouldn't get me addicted
Next thing I knew, I was buying a pack, then two
For the next five years, I struggled to kick the habit
For good
Once you smoke that first cigarette, you're doomed
The nicotine is altering your judgment, placing shackles
Around your wrists

Almost three years ago, I finally quit; it wasn't that hard
Recent events have reignited the habit,
One cigarette here and there
Even now, almost a month clean, and I still crave it
On some animalistic level
The nicotine beckons; I'd like to refuse its call
But I'm weak

# Addicted

I'm happiest when you're talking to me
Opening up and letting me in
Your words are like a drug
A high that was previously unknown to me
I could listen for hours, my attention utterly rapt
I'm not content with just a few; I want them all
They speak in a foreign tongue
Things that I'm unused to hearing
Kind things, loving things
I never knew that one person could
Come into your life and change it so exponentially
You are the sturdy foundation that holds me tall
The loving force that nurtures my soul
You are the axis on which my world turns
I'd be lost without you.

Gabriel Mero

## About The Author

Gabriel Mero is a proud nerd, born and raised in Michigan  Writing has always been a passion of his, starting with fan fictions, and metamorphosing into fiction  He is the author of the *Wildthyme Series*  When not writing, he spends his time showing off his badass pizza making skills, being a cat Dad to his babies, and being a "cousin daddy " On occasion, you might catch him on his YouTube channel "The Literary Madonna," or on his website,

**https://www theliterarymadonna com**

www.ingramcontent.com/pod-product-compliance
Lightning Source LLC
Chambersburg PA
CBHW060326050426
42449CB00011B/2671